Powerful Polar Bears

Charlotte Guillain

Raintree is an imprint of Capstone Global Library Limited, a company incorporated in England and Wales having its registered office at 7 Pilgrim Street, London, EC4V 6LB – Registered company number: 6695582

To contact Raintree:
Phone: 0845 6044371
Fax: + 44 (0) 1865 312263
Email: myorders@raintreepublishers.co.uk
Outside the UK please telephone +44 1865 312262.

Text © Capstone Global Library Limited 2013
First published in hardback in 2013
The moral rights of the proprietor have been asserted.

Edited by Daniel Nunn, Rebecca Rissman, and Catherine Veitch
Designed by Victoria Allen
Picture research by Mica Brancic
Production by Victoria Fitzgerald
Originated by Capstone Global Library Ltd
Printed and bound in China by CTPS

ISBN 978 1 406 26080 9
17 16 15 14 13
10 9 8 7 6 5 4 3 2 1

British Library Cataloguing in Publication Data
Guillain, Charlotte.
Powerful polar bears. -- (Walk on the wild side)
599.7'86-dc23
A full catalogue record for this book is available from the British Library.

Acknowledgements
We would like to thank the following for permission to reproduce photographs: Getty Images pp. 12 (Oxford Scientific/Daniel Cox), 13 (All Canada Photos/Don Johnston), 20 (Peter Arnold/Fred Bruemmer), 26 (Universal Images Group/© Eleanor Briccetti), 28 (Oxford Scientific/Mike Hil), 29 (All Canada Photos/Ron Erwin); Nature Picture Library pp. 7, 24 (both © Andy Rouse), 8, 9, 10, 11, 16, 18, 21, 27 (all © Steven Kazlowski), 14 (© Staffan Widstrand), 17 (© Mats Forsberg), 22 (© Nick Garbutt), 23 (© Eric Baccega); Shutterstock pp. 4 (© Yvonne Pijnenburg-Schonewille), 5 (© Hal Brindley), 15 (© Vlad Ghiea), 19 (© Thomas Barrat), 25 (© Uryadnikov Sergey).

Cover photograph of a polar bear reproduced with permission of FLPA (© Dickie Duckett).

We would like to thank Michael Bright for his invaluable help in the preparation of this book.

Every effort has been made to contact copyright holders of material reproduced in this book. Any omissions will be rectified in subsequent printings if notice is given to the publisher.

All the Internet addresses (URLs) given in this book were valid at the time of going to press. However, due to the dynamic nature of the Internet, some addresses may have changed, or sites may have changed or ceased to exist since publication. While the author and publisher regret any inconvenience this may cause readers, no responsibility for any such changes can be accepted by either the author or the publisher.

Some words are shown in bold, **like this**. You can find out what they mean by looking in the glossary.

Contents

Introducing polar bears

Polar bears are huge white bears that live in the **Arctic**. They are very beautiful but they are also deadly hunters. Polar bears are the largest **carnivores** living on land.

Polar bears spend time both on land and in the sea.

Did you know?

The polar bear's **Latin name**, *Ursus maritimus*, means "sea bear".

Where do polar bears live?

The polar bear's **habitat** includes frozen sea ice, as well as land in the **Arctic** region.

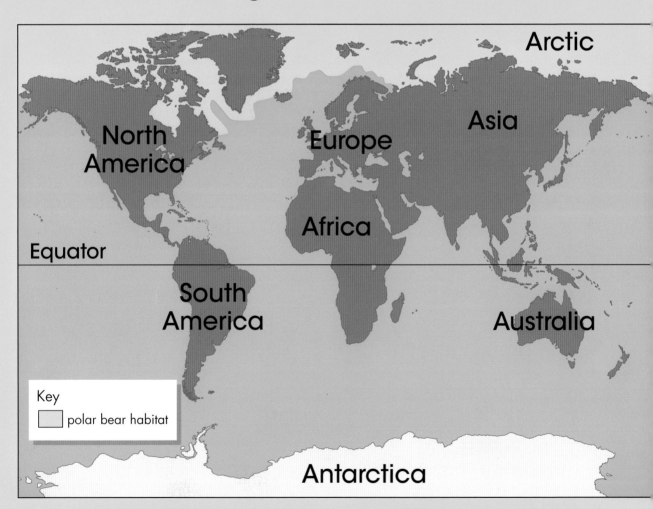

Arctic

North America

Europe

Asia

Africa

Equator

South America

Australia

Key
polar bear habitat

Antarctica

What do polar bears look like?

Polar bears are really big. They can be 3 metres long and weigh up to 680 kilograms. Polar bears have long necks with fairly small heads. Their claws are curved and very strong.

Polar bears' teeth and claws are extremely sharp.

Fur and skin

Polar bears' white fur is **water repellent**. This means water doesn't stay in the fur and freeze. Under the fur is a thick layer of fat, which also keeps the bear warm. The skin under a polar bear's fur is black. Black skin holds any heat from the sun better than paler skin.

black skin

11

Polar bear paws

Polar bears' paws are specially **adapted** for life in the **Arctic**. Fur on the bottom of each paw helps to grip onto the ice as the bear moves around. A polar bear's huge paws help to stop it from sinking into the snow.

Getting around

Polar bears cover huge distances looking for **prey**. They often walk more than 30 kilometres in a day. Polar bears are also very good swimmers. Their front paws are partly **webbed** to help them swim. They can close their nostrils under water.

Did you know?
Polar bears can swim
for 100 kilometres
without stopping.

Hunting

Apart from females with cubs, most polar bears live and hunt alone. Their white fur is good **camouflage** as they hunt on the ice. Polar bears use their camouflage to **stalk prey** without being seen.

Can you spot the polar bear?

seal pup

Did you know?

Polar bears mainly hunt seals, but will also eat birds, walruses, and whales.

Super senses

Polar bears use their excellent sense of smell to find **prey**. They can smell seals from more than 32 kilometres away. Polar bears also have good senses of sight and hearing.

Polar bears can smell a seal's den under thick ice.

Lying in wait

When a polar bear has sniffed out a seal, it often waits near cracks or holes in the ice. When the seal comes up to breathe, the polar bear pounces.

Did you know?
Sometimes polar bears
smash holes in the
ice to find seal pups
underneath.

Scavenging

When the sea ice melts in summer, it is harder for polar bears to hunt seals. Then they **scavenge** to survive. Polar bears will eat dead animals if they find them. They will also raid dustbins in towns.

Polar bears eat berries in autumn.

It can be dangerous for people when polar bears look for food in towns.

23

Polar bear cubs

Female polar bears dig dens deep in the snow to give birth to cubs in winter. The cubs drink their mother's milk, which is rich in fat. Cubs normally stay with their mother for over two years.

Did you know?

Polar bear mothers normally have twins.

Cubs leave the den in March or April.

Learning to swim and hunt

Mother polar bears teach their **cubs** how to hunt. At first the cubs watch. When they are about a year old, they start to hunt for themselves. Mother bears also teach cubs how to swim. Sometimes mothers carry cubs on their backs if they have to swim a long way.

Life for a polar bear

Today polar bears sometimes struggle to find food as the sea ice in the **Arctic** is melting. It is important that humans protect their **habitat**.

Polar bears might look cute. But, remember, they are one of the deadliest **predators** in the world!

Glossary

adapted developed to suit the environment

Arctic polar region in the far north

camouflage colouring or disguise that hides an animal from view

carnivore meat-eater

habitat natural home for an animal or plant

predator animal that kills and eats other animals

prey animal killed by another animal for food

scavenge look for dead animals or rubbish for food

stalk creep up on

water repellent does not soak up water

webbed having skin between toes to act as a paddle when swimming

Find out more

Books

Face to Face with Polar Bears, Norbert Rosing (National Geographic, 2009)

Polar Bears and their Homes, Angela Royston (First Facts Books, 2010)

Polar Bear vs. Seal, Mary Meinking (Raintree, 2012)

The Polar Regions' Most Amazing Animals, Anita Ganeri (Raintree, 2008)

Websites

gowild.wwf.org.uk/regions/polar-fact-files/polar-bear
The World Wildlife Fund website has a fact file on polar bears.

kids.nationalgeographic.com/kids/animals/creaturefeature/polar-bear/
The National Geographic website has information on many animals, including polar bears.

www.globio.org/glossopedia/article.aspx?art_id=77&art_nm=Polar+Bears
Find out more about polar bears.

Index